Distributed ELINT Collection Marrying Electronic Warfare with Intelligence, Surveillance, and Reconnaissance to Broaden Collection and Provide Global Situational Awareness

John T. Todd

This is a curated and comprehensive collection of the most important works covering matters related to national security, diplomacy, defense, war, strategy, and tactics. The collection spans centuries of thought and experience, and includes the latest analysis of international threats, both conventional and asymmetric. It also includes riveting first person accounts of historic battles and wars.

Some of the books in this Series are reproductions of historical works preserved by some of the leading libraries in the world. As with any reproduction of a historical artifact, some of these books contain missing or blurred pages, poor pictures, errant marks, etc. We believe these books are essential to this collection and the study of war, and have therefore brought them back into print, despite these imperfections.

We hope you enjoy the unmatched breadth and depth of this collection, from the historical to the just-published works.

AIR COMMAND AND STAFF COLLEGE

AIR UNIVERSITY

DISTRIBUTED ELINT COLLECTION

MARRYING ELECTRONIC WARFARE (EW) WITH INTELLIGENCE, SURVEILLANCE, AND RECONNAISSANCE (ISR) TO BROADEN COLLECTION AND PROVIDE GLOBAL SITUATIONAL AWARENESS

by

John T. Todd, Major, USAF

A Research Report Submitted to the Faculty

In Partial Fulfillment of the Graduation Requirements

Instructor: Maj Julie Verdura

Maxwell Air Force Base, Alabama

April 2006

Disclaimer

The views expressed in this academic research paper are those of the author(s) and do not reflect the official policy or position of the US government or the Department of Defense. In accordance with Air Force Instruction 51-303, it is not copyrighted, but is the property of the United States government.

ABSTRACT

Today's Intelligence, Surveillance and Reconnaissance (ISR) collection and distribution architecture has evolved from disparate developmental efforts from the services and Intelligence Community. Interoperability and responsiveness problems in this architecture were highlighted in 1991, during Operation DESERT STORM. For the past 15 years, the Department of Defense and Intelligence Community have undergone many improvement efforts. These improvements are leading to greater interoperability, greater bandwidth, and greater sensor technology.

Improvements in information sharing provide an essential foundation for a new approach to ELINT collection. The efforts made in improving connectivity, interoperability and sensor capability enable a new Electronics Intelligence (ELINT) collection architecture. A network of tactical aircraft Electronic Warfare (EW) receiver systems holds the potential to broaden the field and depth of view of current ISR platforms. This networked sensor quilt would provide ELINT information from multiple perspectives and add to the quality of the Operational ELINT (OPELINT) picture. This ELINT architecture would provide a common picture for global situational awareness to warfighters and command and control elements of all of the services.

Although the priority on Human Intelligence (HUMINT), Imagery Intelligence (IMINT), and Communications Intelligence (COMINT) required for the Global War on Terrorism might divert focus from improvements in ELINT collection and distribution, there are some steps needed to lay the foundation for distributed ELINT collection. Efforts to enable a horizontal architecture for distributed ELINT information would serve well to meet the goal of information superiority espoused by Network Centric Warfare advocates and called for by Joint Vision 2010 and 2020.

INTRODUCTION

Electronics Intelligence (ELINT) in the United States military and Intelligence Community is facing challenges with evolving from its current architecture to one which best takes advantage of the capabilities available with new information sharing technologies. Since the Operation DESERT STORM campaign in 1991, the US military has made remarkable improvements in the ability to collect and move intelligence information quickly to the warfighter. Datalinks and broadcast video feeds have significantly increased situational awareness of those on the battlefield and the command and control elements orchestrating campaigns. The military services have begun transforming to implement information distribution systems. These advances have led to a significant increase in intelligence collection and distribution capability. However, the advances made in distributing information have been occurring at a frenzied pace which has led to each of the services and intelligence agencies scrambling to develop intelligence systems to take advantage of the technology advances. The pace of the advances has also led to services developing piecemeal network technologies without a broad joint strategy guiding the acquisition of these systems to ensure interoperability.

As a result of this piecemeal approach, today's Intelligence, Surveillance, and Reconnaissance (ISR) networks suffer from many problems with interoperability. Once the information is gathered, it is distributed through stove-piped networks. That is the networks are very vertically structured with a few collectors feeding into a few or even a single node for analysis and then redistributed to the users. The end users are generally a small group of similar type weapons systems or command and control agencies. The large number of networks and data links that carry similar information is evidence of this stove-piped architecture. Until recently, many of these ISR networks were incompatible because they were developed by each of the services to accomplish specific tasks for those links and then counted on other communications methods for moving the information beyond the datalink. This was the result of a failure to take a systematic view of the collection and distribution of the data across all potential users. However, the military and intelligence communities have noticed the need to improve interoperability, and are attempting to provide a common strategy to the distribution of information.

Another problem with distributing information is the network architectures were laid over the existing collection and communication systems' architecture. This architecture relies heavily on older collection platforms to gather the information. Because many of these systems are aging, they require ongoing improvement programs to remain capable collection platforms. Therefore, the information networking programs have had to compete with resources for platform improvements. The networks associated with ISR collectors have often needed to be overhauled when the collection systems were upgraded.

Current Network Centric Warfare (NCW) efforts in ISR equipment acquisition and upgrades are making progress on improving compatibility of collection and distribution systems. One of the main goals of NCW is ensuring interoperability of systems. Many current NCW initiatives involve increasing interoperability of information systems among the services and coalition partners[1]. Another key tenet of NCW is all battlefield entities: platforms, sensors, and shooters should be made net ready, which means they are built with the communications equipment necessary to connect to communications datalinks.[2] The focus on making platforms net ready has started to pay off with the F-22A Raptor and the F-35 Joint Strike Fighter (JSF). These tactical aircraft are leveraging their connectivity to facilitate sharing of information among their avionics and sensors in an unprecedented way. This connectivity will be discussed in greater

2

detail later. The services are beginning to embrace transformation along the lines of NCW. Their work is aimed at increasing the interoperability of interservice and intraservice networks. This should lead to increased horizontal information sharing capability for all types of ISR and command and control broadcasts.

This paper will not argue whether or not NCW is needed, but rather will focus on a specific potential application of NCW. That application is one of a networked ELINT sensor quilt. The paper will highlight the shortfalls of today's ELINT architecture, examine some of the efforts underway to address these shortcomings, and expand the current architecture through networked Electronic Warfare (EW) systems. Next, the paper will explore the feasibility and constraints of implementing the specific network centric application of a distributed network of ELINT sensors and processors to provide battlespace awareness to the aircraft in theater and the headquarters elements that command and control them. Finally, this paper will examine the feasibility of such an effort in light of the ongoing Global War on Terrorism and recommend some measures to be taken now to establish the necessary infrastructure for enabling such a sensor network when it does become feasible.

CURRENT SHORTFALLS

During Operation IRAQI FREEDOM (OIF), limitations were exposed in the ability for airborne ISR and command and control assets to provide timely, accurate, fused, and actionable intelligence.[3] In his research paper for Naval War College detailing the challenges of ISR in OIF, Lieutenant Commander Carl M. Bradley noted, "These C4ISR challenges resulted from the extreme speed of maneuvers, incompatible and service-unique C4ISR systems, distributed command structures, and the chasm between the huge amounts of raw information being collected by sensors and the *OIF* intelligence effort's ability to direct, collect, exploit, analyze, and disseminate fused intelligence products."[4]

The interoperability challenge of ISR sytems has been identified for at least 15 years. In 1997, the Defense Science Board Task Force on Command, Control, Communications, Computers, Intelligence, Surveillance, and Reconnaissance (C4ISR) noted these interoperability problems in their final report.[5] Their report explained the services, in an attempt to provide the C4ISR to meet each of their needs, ended up creating systems lacking sufficient integration. The Defense Science Board noted there were efforts ongoing to rectify the issues, but believed these efforts were not adequate and lacked the proper level of oversight to overcome these deficiencies in integration.[6]

Although the services and Intelligence Community's development and acquisition processes made some improvements in achieving integration and interoperability in the last decade, there continued to be problems with formal oversight of the process. Evidence of this problem can be seen in a May 2003 Senate Select Committee on Intelligence report. The committee noted they were "aware of no capability within the DOD or the Intelligence Community for objectively, independently, and comprehensively evaluating alternative sensor and platform architecture and capabilities. There are some capabilities within different agencies and departments, but none are available, independent of the program offices, to model and assess cross-program trades without regard to the location of the sensor or platform (air, space, land, or sea) or the level of compartmentation(sic). Consequently, although DOD and Intelligence Community officials expend substantial effort and time evaluating program trades, they do so without the benefit of the rigorous quantitative modeling necessary to optimize collection capabilities and architectures. "[7] In his statement before the Senate Armed Services Committee's Strategic

Forces Subcommittee, Dr. Stephen A. Cambone, Undersecretary of Defense for Intelligence, gave some of the blame for this lack of cohesion to organization and doctrine for ISR which "has not been systematically revised for two generations. ISR activities are burdened by legacy policies and stove-piped activities which are de-conflicted, but not integrated..."[8] With this lack of unity of effort, it should not be a surprise that incompatibility was exposed in the intelligence systems in OIF. It is instead rather remarkable the systems had even modest levels of integration.

Although ELINT collection and dissemination systems are becoming increasingly networked, these systems continue to suffer from an architecture which imposes other constraints. One of the inherent problems with today's ELINT architecture is the reliance on a few collectors to provide the total Operational ELINT (OPELINT) picture for the Joint Operations Area (JOA). SIGINT is usually collected from many methods, but the airborne SIGINT collection platforms are usually a few aircraft dedicated to gathering signals. OPELINT collectors include ground, air, and satellite systems. These systems are designed to collect high fidelity information on signals intercepts. The information collected from these systems is used to locate, identify, and potentially target enemy systems. This information is sent back to analysts usually in the rear or Continental United States (CONUS). From there, it is redistributed to command and control elements and tactical entities through intelligence broadcasts or voice.

The process of distributing OPELINT data is fairly mature through intelligence broadcasts to battlespace entities equipped to receive the signals. However, many tankers, transport, and special operations aircraft flying in the JOA are unable to receive these broadcasts. Currently most ISR and command and control elements are equipped to receive the OPELINT datalinks.

Entities such as the Combined Air Operations Center (CAOC), Distributed Common Ground System (DCGS), and most headquarters intelligence sections are equipped to receive intelligence information. The DCGS allows for economy of force for intelligence analysts by providing a single source for capturing collected SIGINT as well as other intelligence information from the Area of Operation (AO). DCGS crews analyze the data and publish products for general consumption throughout the AO in response to specific analysis requests.

Today's air breathing OPELINT collectors are capable aircraft with proven ability to locate and identify threat systems. However they are neither infallible nor omnipresent. The idea of recalling an entire air package due to the loss of an ELINT collection asset seems far fetched when considered in the context of the past few major combat operations, but might be the correct decision when facing a threat with modern Integrated Air Defense Systems (IADS) and mobile Surface-to-Air Missiles (SAM) such as SA-10s and SA-20s. Airborne SIGINT collection platforms such as the RC-135 Rivet Joint will be necessary to provide threat awareness during such operations. Because they are crucial and limited in numbers, these few collection platforms represent critical nodes in airborne operations.

However, even when ELINT collectors are present, there is no guarantee of complete situational awareness. This was illustrated with the shoot down of the F-117 in Kosovo. Benjamin Lambeth in his report, "Strategic and Operational Assessment of NATO's Air War in Kosovo" for Rand's Project Air Force, concluded one of the contributing factors to the shootdown was the inability to locate and track the offending surface to air missile (SAM) Batteries.[9]

Besides the OPELINT picture, virtually all tactical aircraft are equipped with Electronic Warfare (EW) receivers to provide Tactical ELINT (TACELINT) threat warning. The receivers generally collect less information about the signals it receives than OPELINT platforms, and processes the information into general threat information for aircrews. Electronic Attack (EA) systems, designed to jam threat radars, also usually have a receiver subsystem that collects signal information necessary to effectively counter radar systems. These receiver subsystems vary on the amount of information (if any) that is provided to the aircrew. On more modern aircraft the EA receiver subsystem also serves as the TACELINT receiver. TACELINT information is generally not widely disseminated but may be passed to other aircraft by means of voice communication. This method of dissemination is based on commonly used brevity terms. Although these brevity terms make the communication fairly quick, the amount and fidelity of the information transferred about the signal is limited. Furthermore, this data is generally not recorded for future exploitation. TACELINT data may be presented in post flight reports but this data suffers from the constraints of the aircrew's ability to recall the receiver data and their geospatial data at the time of reception.

With this background on the current ELINT architecture some constraints are readily apparent. OPELINT suffers from the limitations of distribution system interoperability and collection assets availability and capability. Even when all collection assets are brought to bear, there is seldom 24 hour persistence. Furthermore, collection assets capabilities may not ensure collection of Low Probability of Intercept (LPI) or signals with small beamwidths. Both OPELINT and TACELINT consist of similar information about the signal parameters, source identity, and location of signals TACELINT contains less comprehensive data about the signal and suffers from a lack of networking capability altogether. Therefore it is not collected and stored information and is usually known to only one entity. Usually, only OPELINT is broadcast and analyzed by more than one entity. OPELINT collection capability and network interoperability are being continuously improved. TACELINT receivers and EA systems are also becoming more capable, but only a few programs have started to distribute this information.

IMPROVEMENT EFFORTS

Many improvements to the capabilities of OPELINT collection efforts have been ongoing in an attempt to keep up with the challenges of modern signal environment. Although the fleet of ISR platforms is aging, current efforts should extend their service until at least the 2020's.[10] These efforts are necessary to ensure the platforms are capable of providing comprehensive information of modern radar signals in an ever denser signal environment. Equally important to improvements in the capabilities of the collection platforms are improvements in their ability to distribute the information effectively.

Current efforts are underway to improve the ISR process. These improvements focus largely on overcoming problems with interoperability, improving collection capability of current platforms and improving broadcast bandwidth availability. The work to improve interoperability has come from two main efforts. The first consists of creating a standard for SIGINT information to which all collection and distribution systems can adhere. This step is critical for the networking of SIGINT systems and attempts to eliminate the proliferation of many separate networks each devising their own protocols and data standards. The second effort involves creating common equipment between the services to eliminate redundancy and ensure interoperability. Although work to make a common standard for SIGINT data is fairly mature the process of acquiring equipment for all services to employ has had limited success.

The effort to create a common architecture for SIGINT data collection and dissemination was formalized in mid 1990s with the creation of the Joint SIGINT Working Group (JSWG). One of the main missions of the JSWG was the creation of the Joint Airborne SIGINT

Architecture (JASA). JASA was developed to meet the promise of an open architecture for information dominance spelled out in Joint Vision 2010.[11]

JASA's open architecture allows for newly developed equipment to be introduced into the network without having to build an extra interface system. Another characteristic of JASA is that it calls for digitization of signals early in the reception path. This early digitization of signals allows for ease of processing and communication of digital signals with modern electronics. Early digitization also requires fewer amplification components of a receiver system. Other key components of the JASA framework include high bandwidth local area networks, interface standards to ensure connectivity of various configurations, optimal use of commercial off the shelf technology and security safeguards throughout the system.[12]

The main benefit JASA provides is a common framework to implement new technology for SIGINT collection and distribution systems. The framework would apply to the whole SIGINT community across the services and would address many of the problems of interoperability from service components of the SIGINT process. However this standard applies only to airborne SIGINT collection assets. Fortunately, there have been similar efforts to ensure standards within the communication of SIGINT from maritime and overhead assets.

More recently, efforts have been made to move beyond these standards in improving interoperability of ISR collection and distribution systems. The 2004 Defense Authorization Act created the Intelligence Surveillance and Reconnaissance Integration Council (ISRIC) with the charge of ensuring interoperability among the ISR assets for each of the services.[13] The ISRIC is comprised of the senior intelligence officers from the services and United States Special Operations Command (USSOCOM); the Director of Operations of the Joint Staff; and the directors of the Department of Defense (DOD) intelligence agencies. The council is tasked with assisting the Undersecretary of Defense for Intelligence with integration of ISR and coordinating development activities of the military departments, intelligence agencies of the DOD and relevant commands. The ISRIC was further tasked to create a comprehensive plan to guide development and integration of DOD ISR capabilities for the 15 fiscal year period of 2004 through 2018. This comprehensive guide is the "Defense Intelligence, Surveillance, and Reconnaissance Integration Roadmap."

Building on interoperability efforts are improvements in datalinks and network bandwidth capability. The Global Information Grid (GIG) represents a main thrust to improve connectivity throughout the Department of Defense. This effort lays the foundation for information sharing in the future. Although progress is being made in implementation of the GIG, the effort faces challenges of deciding when, how, and how much information should be put on the network.[14] Until ISR collection and distribution systems become completely compliant with the GIG architecture, improvements in bandwidth and interoperability of current datalinks will be necessary.

Although JASA standards and the ISR Integration Council represent the DOD's real commitment to incorporating interoperability into its development activities, the recent cancellation of the Aerial Common Sensor (ACS) represents a setback. The Aerial Common Sensor was a joint effort with the US Army as the lead. It was designed to incorporate several ISR intelligence sensors into a single integrated platform. It was designed to provide wide area surveillance through Imagery, Signals and Measures and Signals Intelligence (IMINT, SIGINT, and MASINT) sensors.[15] ACS included multiple datalinks to communicate with command and control entities such as the in-theater DCGS-A as well as datalink connectivity with Airborne command and control and ISR collection aircraft as well as tactical strike aircraft through Link-

16. Additionally, ACS was designed to incorporate datalink connectivity with Unmanned Aerial Systems (UASs) to provide a distribution node for their data and potentially extend their effective operating range.[16] ACS was designed to replace the Army's Guardrail and Airborne Reconnaissance-Low (ARL) systems which were neither fully networked nor integrated. However ACS was more than just a combination of the existing systems with network capability it would incorporate new technologies and a much more robust set of sensors to provide battlespace awareness.

Although the halting of the ACS program is a setback to ISR integration efforts, it may well be a sign integration and interoperability efforts are truly working. According to Claude Bolton, Assistant Secretary of the Army for Acquisition Logistics and Technology, it was "decided that the prudent course of action at this time was to terminate the contract and bring the various players industry, the acquisition and user communities, the Navy and Air Force back to the drawing board to make sure we all have a firm understanding of what the requirements are and the various challenges we need to overcome to make this program succeed. We are not terminating the program."[17] Regardless of the intentions of halting the ACS program, the impact is the legacy Guardrail and ARL programs will have to bear some burden of SIGINT collection in the near term. This in turn means more networked SIGINT distribution is pushed farther into the future.

One of the most important investments currently underway to bolster the US military's ELINT capabilities lies in the EW technology being imbedded in new aircraft. The F-22A Raptor and F-35 Joint Strike Fighter (JSF) have an unprecedented capability to collect and distribute ELINT information. The F-22A leverages a passive surveillance system built into the airframe providing a very capable ELINT collection capability. The F-22A maximizes use of passive systems to ensure stealth. According to the 1995 Defense Science Board Task Force report entitled "Concurrency and Risk of the F-22 Program", the F-22 has "Multiple (15-20) sources of passive surveillance designed to: Provide situational awareness – Minimize active (radar) [parenthesis in original] emissions – Provide identification. – Cue defensive measures, weapons, Electronic Warfare (EW), flares"[18] Furthermore, the F-22A also has the datalink capability to distribute this information to other battlespace entities.

According to Loren Thompson, vice president of the Lexington Institute, a think tank in Arlington Virginia, "The Raptor combines the ability to pick up electromagnetic emissions across a broad spectrum…with a pair of powerful onboard computers with a vast library of signal patterns. This allows the aircraft to collect, process, and identify signals in a way no other fighter aircraft can."[19] Ray Goodson, senior manager of the Integrated Warfare Development Center (IWDC) at Lockheed Martin Aeronautics' Fort Worth, Tex., facility, was quoted as saying "the sensor suite is almost as powerful as that of many advanced electronic intelligence (ELINT) gathering aircraft, for signal identification capability and pinpointing subjects with precision."[20]

The F-22A represents a step forward in the integration and dissemination of tactical sensor data on fighter aircraft. The JSF program leverages much of the technology developed for the F-22A. According to John Waldrop, Lockheed Martin's International Programs director, the JSF will have similar ISR capabilities.[21] Most of the details regarding the F-22A's capability in comparison to dedicated ELINT platforms remains classified, and the comments from contractors might be misleading. However, the F-22A represents a breakthrough not so much for its ability to locate and identify threats, but rather its ability to fuse that data with other sensor data, provide it to the pilot in a meaningful way, and disseminate it outside of the aircraft.

Loren Thompson cautions, "No sensor system is better in aperture, power supply or field of view than the platform carrying it." The Raptor "will never have the field of view of a satellite and never be able to eavesdrop with the depth of a Rivet Joint."[22] This may be true, but one could envision a fleet of similar aircraft flying throughout the battlespace each providing a portion of the ELINT picture. At a given moment in time this as a whole could have a total field of view of a satellite and have even greater depth than an RC-135 Rivet Joint. This marrying of individual aircraft EW systems into an ISR collection network represents a potential solution to many of the challenges the ELINT collection community faces.

The EW world is beginning to grasp the potential of distributed ELINT information and is developing concepts for more traditional EW systems. One example of this is the ALR-69A(v) Radar Warning Receiver (RWR). The ALR-69A(v) is a follow-on system based on the ALR-69(v) currently employed on Air Force Special Operations Command (AFSOC), and some F-16 aircraft. The new ALR-69A(v) is in the final stages of development and flight testing and should enter production this year.[23] The system represents an increase in capability in precision location and identification of threat systems. However more intriguing is a Defense Advanced Research Projects Agency (DARPA) technology demonstration using the new receiver system. DARPA plans to use the ALR-69A(v) in a Advanced Tactical Targeting Technology (AT3) demonstration in 2007. The demonstration will use three F-16 Block 30 aircraft fitted with networked ALR-69A(V) systems to triangulate the location of threat systems. The AT3 demonstration is designed to show the capability of networked systems to rapidly and accurately locate RF emitters without assistance from other ELINT gathering platforms.[24] The location of the emitter is accomplished by "using time difference of arrival and frequency difference of arrival measurements by multiple RWRs. Rather than using dedicated SIGINT or EW systems,

AT3 would pinpoint the location of an enemy SAM surveillance or fire-control radar by fusing information from the RWRs of any U.S. tactical aircraft flying in a given area."[25]

The advances in ELINT collection capability and integrated communications networks offer a brief glimpse at the solutions the military is exploring to overcome the problems with interoperability, stove-piped network architectures and modern signal collection difficulties. Further, the networked sensor technology of the F-22A and JSF, as well as the networked RWR technologies being explored by DARPA, represent the foundation for a future ELINT network architecture providing a leap forward in capability.

ELINT SENSOR QUILT AS A SOLUTION

As previously alluded to, one solution to the limitations of both TACELINT and OPELINT would be to equip all aircraft entities with high fidelity receivers and network them to provide a common picture of the combined ELINT data. These receivers would likely already be incorporated in most platforms as Radar Warning Receivers (RWRs) or as receiver subsystems of Electronic Attack (EA) systems. OPELINT would gain a broader coverage, multiple perspectives and more precision in locating emitters. Furthermore, the quality of ELINT would increase. One example of a qualitative information gain is that a networked ELINT sensor quilt would also be able to identify which aircraft are currently being targeted by threat systems. This information is currently available, but only via voice communication from the targeted aircraft. Furthermore, small beamwidth and low power signals that current OPELINT collectors may miss are more likely to be captured by a collaborative collection network.

As stated earlier, TACELINT data is usually not communicated or recorded. If it is shared, it is done so through voice communications and brevity words. The speed and quality of this data could greatly be increased with a network of multiple sensors. The networking of

14

TACELINT platforms would add depth and quality to the OPELINT picture as well as providing critical information to tactical aircraft. The lead aircraft in a formation could easily determine which aircraft was being targeted, by which system and what the geospatial relationship is to each aircraft. This ability should lead to new defensive tactics or formation geometries which maximize mutual support.

The ability to provide an ELINT sensor quilt providing global situational awareness relies on several enabling factors. First, the system must have the ability to communicate signal data. In other words the data must be transferable from one entity to another. Furthermore the data should be transferred digitally so as to provide the ability for modern processors on each end to use and display the data. The ability to transfer data from aircraft to aircraft is one of the most significant improvements for air power in the past decade. Much of this capability has come in the form of datalinks for fighter aircraft and imagery distribution networks for ISR asset. Because TACELINT contains essentially the same signal data as OPELINT, the addition of TACELINT into a combined broadcast should only require an increase in bandwidth for the existing network architecture. Moreover, JASA standards for SIGINT networks set the framework for an ELINT sensor quilt network.

The ability to process received signals to determine the type of signal is another necessary factor in developing a global SA network. However there are at least two ways of processing information. The first method of processing signals is to have each of the sensor systems combined with their own processor subsystems. This option adds the complexity, weight, and expense of several processors. Another method would be to communicate raw signal data to a single or few processing nodes which process data and retransmit results to all entities on the network. This method ensures a common picture to all users, but carries the risk of a critical vulnerability to the system and lack of timeliness and is therefore undesirable. Currently most receivers have some rudimentary processing capability. It would make sense to retain this processing capability inherent in each aircraft. With a distributed processing capability comes redundancy and responsiveness.

The real promise of a truly distributed TACELINT sensor quilt is the force enabler of global situational awareness. Global situational awareness implies the ability to not only know your own position in relation to other aircraft and the enemy, but also the ability to know which aircraft are being targeted by the enemy as well as threat location. Displaying active threat systems with a relative position to an aircraft will allow greater flexibility for strike or air superiority aircraft. The increased visibility of potential threats gives greater time to adjust routing and attack profiles.

The ability to target offending threat systems while providing mutual support to a defending aircraft would be very beneficial. According to the US Air Force Transformation Flight Plan of 2004, the ability to retarget strike aircraft has significantly increased since Operation DESERT STORM. During DESERT STORM, about 20 percent of the sorties received their targets or had their targets changed after take-off. This increased to 43 percent in Operation ALLIED FORCE and 80 percent in Operation ENDURING FREEDOM. The Flight plan estimated 90 percent of the sorties in Operation IRAQI FREEDOM responded to targeting after take-off.[26] The transformation flight plan contributes this increase to "The improved integration of sensors, networks and the TPED (Tasking Processing Exploitation and Dissemination... definition added) process..."[27] One could argue which of these three enablers contributed the most to the dynamic retasking of air assets. However, it is clear the ability to respond to information well within the ATO cycle has become an important part of the way the Air Force operates. A networked

ELINT sensor quilt contributing to the overall common operating should enhance this capability.

One ISR limitation that the sensor quilt would not cure is that of interoperability. The Interoperability problems outlined earlier would hamper the distribution of a comprehensive ELINT network just as it hampers the distribution systems today. Solving the ISR network interoperability problems must be a part of creating an effective battlespace awareness picture for all users. The NCW solutions to interoperability currently underway should enable the sharing of information to all air, ground, maritime, and command and control users.

The Quadrennial Defense Review (QDR) released February 6, 2006 sends mixed messages relating to future implementation of a horizontal ELINT distribution architecture. On one hand, the QDR emphasizes a reachback approach to ISR architectures which leverages reserve forces and reduces the footprint of forward deployed forces. Focusing on reachback tends to reinforce an architecture relying on a few critical nodes and thus propagating one of the problems in the current architecture. This focus emphasizes the ability to take information from multiple collection sources and analyze the collected data at a single location to which all units can reach back for products to answer their intelligence concerns. While the focus on reachback does imply a limited number of analysis nodes it does not necessarily imply a limited number of collection entities. On the other hand the QDR emphasizes a sensor based approach which will lead to procurement of much of the necessary infrastructure needed for a horizontal architecture.

The QDR states, "The future force will define ISR needs by sensor or type of intelligence needed rather than the platforms that carry the sensors or the medium in which they operate. This approach will facilitate the substitution of one capability for another to achieve the same effect, and will allow the suppliers of sensor capability to meet the needs of Combatant Commanders more efficiently. This sensor-centric approach will also improve the ability to integrate data horizontally across sensor inputs, thereby ensuring that information is available on a timely basis to a much wider range of users."[28] The emphasis on sensor rather than platform fits well with a horizontal distribution of ELINT data. The emphasis is having the capability to collect the information regardless of the airframe. However it falls short of advocating a leveraging of sensors already incorporated in these aircraft including RWR sensors and receiver subsystems of Electronic Attack (EA) systems. Although these programs illustrate the potential creation of a sensor quilt architecture, the future weight of effort for such an network is in doubt due to the current DOD focus on terrorism.

GLOBAL WAR ON TERRORISM (GWOT) IMPACT

Today's Global War on Terrorism is testing all of the Intelligence Community. The Intelligence Community has undergone radical reform since September 11, 2001 in an effort to reorganize and transform from an entity designed for the Cold War. In this war on terrorism, Human Intelligence (HUMINT) and Communications Intelligence (COMINT) are receiving much of the attention. They represent the focus for improvements and spending in the restructuring of the Intelligence Community. Improvements in these two disciplines are obvious and necessary to fight the current war. Spending a great deal of capital and effort to quickly improve ELINT capability would be unwarranted. While the current shortfalls of the armed forces ELINT capabilities need to be addressed, the benefits of completely overhauling the ELINT architecture would not be a high priority.

The distributed ELINT sensor quilt envisioned in this paper requires a large investment for today's aircraft. While the benefits of this investment have been highlighted in the previous section, the US military today has an unprecedented capability in providing battlespace awareness to warfighters. Completely overhauling the ELINT architecture should not be a top priority when the Intelligence Community has other challenges to overcome. While beneficial, the upgrading of current aircraft with the infrastructure necessary to create a web of ELINT sensors is probably not appropriate while we continue to fight the Global War on Terror.

Although this paper has attempted to describe the potential benefits of a collaborative network of TACELINT and OPELINT sensors, these benefits may not be applicable to fighting a dispersed enemy without borders or conventional forces. The benefits would be most applicable to a foe with a robust air defense system. Furthermore, should we confront a formidable air defense it is likely the rival power has learned the lessons from DESERT STORM to the present on how the US wages war. That is to say, Strategic Surface to Air Missiles (SAMs) remaining in fixed locations should not be the expected norm in any future war. Rather, the US should be ready to defeat an increasingly mobile and dynamic defense system. In a fight with a dynamic IADS, the air force will have to rely on stealth and the ability to quickly respond to threat systems as they arise. An integrated ELINT network could enable quickly assessing the dynamic battlespace and aid in the targeting and destruction of the enemy's defenses. While the benefits of a distributed ELINT battle picture are significant, they are tempered by the economic realities of the current war on terrorism. However, there are steps that should be taken today to set the framework for a future ELINT network.

RECOMMMENDATIONS

Although the likelihood of facing a near rival state in the near term is low, it likely the Intelligence Community will not have as long as four years to change again to engage major combat operations with a rival threat. Therefore many of the enabling capabilities for creating a distributed ELINT sensor quilt should be pursued as a part of ISR acquisition activities. Although an effort to retrofit all current aircraft in the inventory with equipment to collect, distribute, and display ELINT information would be unrealistic, there are a number of measures which can be taken in the near future to leverage current capabilities and improve the distribution of ELINT data.

The fact that much of the equipment and infrastructure for employing a distributed ELINT sensor architecture does not yet exist in today's aircraft acts as a major barrier to implementing a distributed network. As long as new systems are developed without the necessary equipment or capability to contribute to a sensor network, the barrier will remain in place. Network Centric advocates will continue to push for more horizontal architecture and bandwidth among communication networks. The US military should capitalize on these efforts by making infrastructure investments now.

New manned and unmanned aircraft should be designed with the capability to share ELINT information. To accommodate this, all new aircraft should be equipped with datalink capability. This networking follows the efforts for information superiority outlined in Joint Vision 2020 and should continue to be emphasized along with other NCW acquisition goals.[29] Simply networking aircraft will aid in the distribution of collected information, but also outfitting these aircraft with sensors is necessary to spread the collection capability and achieve the global picture.

In order to realize this global picture, all new manned and unmanned aircraft should be designed with robust sensor packages including ELINT sensors except for the smallest tactical UAS's for which extra sensors would be impractical. These sensors may be in the form of lightweight pods tailorable to different mission sets.

Additionally all new RWR systems should be designed to integrate into a network of similar systems. This means all new RWR and EA systems should include the ability to output their data digitally. This data should include received signal information and direction of arrival. This data combined with geospatial and timing data will be crucial to developing an ELINT battlespace picture. In addition, new RWR systems should incorporate a programmable "God's 'eye'" display capable of providing situational awareness from other aircraft. The combination of all of these recommendations will put into place the necessary infrastructure to implement a distributed ELINT sensor quilt and ensure, when such a system is implemented, it will have few barriers.

Even if these infrastructure measures are put into place today there will still be a need to rely on current architecture to pass much of the ELINT information to today's legacy aircraft. Therefore, there will still be a great need for voice distribution of Imminent Threat Warning (ITW) from ELINT collectors and command and control elements. The U.S Air Force Transformation flight plan calls for greater machine–to-machine information exchange and as the networked ELINT systems replace today's systems the reliance on voice communication should decrease.[30]

As individual EW and ELINT receivers become more capable and machine-to-machine communication becomes the norm for data distribution, the need for dedicated manned ELINT collection platforms to support air operations will be reduced. An effective overall battlespace ELINT picture will be available any time there are aircraft throughout the JOA. Furthermore, air operations would be much less impacted by fallout of these assets. Instead these platforms can focus on directed ISR tasking and deep shaping ISR activities.

CONCLUSION

Although there are advocates and critics of Network Centric Warfare concepts, the US military has embarked on a path to distributing unprecedented levels of information to the lowest levels in an effort to increase situational awareness at all levels. This increased battlefield

awareness holds the promise of enabling warfighters to act within the decision cycle of the

enemy. As each of the services developed new systems to distribute battlefield awareness, they

have unfortunately developed several separate networking solutions. These divergent networks

have been crucial to disseminating certain bits of information needed to enable these warriors to

prosecute their part of the campaign. However, as the idea of sharing and integrating these

disparate sets of information into a common operating picture for everyone has taken hold, the

different networks act as a constraint to a truly integrated and interoperable network. The

networks designed for collecting and distributing ELINT data are just one of the challenges

which need to be overcome to create a combined and integrated common battlespace awareness

picture.

Lack of integration and interoperability is just one of the challenges facing the ELINT

community. Today's ELINT collection platforms are aging and their systems are being

challenged by today's dense signal environment. These systems have difficulty receiving

modern waveforms and LPI signals specifically designed to be difficult to intercept.

ELINT collection is neither sufficiently persistent nor effectively distributed to all battlefield

users. OPELINT information is dependant upon the presence of limited collectors. Once

collected, ELINT information is distributed to a few nodes in the rear area or in the United States

before it is distributed in theater. Once distributed, only a few battlefield entities have the ability

to receive the information digitally. Many aircraft still rely on voice communication and brevity

terms to send and receive pertinent ELINT information.

Despite the challenges with today's ELINT architecture, the United States military has made

great improvements in collecting and sharing information of all kinds. Collection problems are being addressed with the acquisition of upgraded collection equipment. The problem with stove-piped networks unable to communicate from service to service has been identified and efforts are underway to correct them. JASA and other standards have created interoperable frameworks from which integrated networks can be based. Improvements in bandwidth and more commonality among datalinks are also countering problems of interoperability.

However, current ELINT improvement efforts do little more than address current identified shortfalls. Truly horizontal networking solutions hold the promise of unleashing even more potential from ELINT systems. Focusing on communicating and displaying ELINT data among battlefield entities should enable greater flexibility in responding to future dynamic air defense systems.

Distributing the collection of ELINT data from a few collectors to virtually all airborne aircraft is common in today's military, but taking the next step to distributing the total ELINT picture from both EW and ISR platforms crucial to unlocking the entire potential for ELINT battlespace awareness. Distributing the collection of ELINT enables more precision in locating signals, collection in the deep battlespace and less reliance on voice communication for ITW. The ability to know the location and the intended target of all active threat systems in a target area would also allow for more secure attack profiles and mutual support in defense.

Finally this paper illustrates one small portion of the information collection and distribution transformation currently taking place within the DOD and the Intelligence Community. An effort to create a common operating picture developed from all intelligence disciplines continues. IMINT, including real time video, has already seen some of the greatest gains in interoperability and distribution. HUMINT and COMINT will continue to receive a great deal of focus for the GWOT. This leaves ELINT as the discipline with the least visibility and effort. However, a truly integrated and distributed ELINT architecture would provide a much needed force enabler for major combat operations with a modern IADS. The effort to integrate each of the sensor entities into a networked web promises to add to the instantaneous field of view, depth of view, and better precision from multiple perspectives. With this total picture of the battlespace, commanders and warfighters alike will have better situational awareness to prosecute tomorrow's campaigns.

NOTES

1 US Department of Defense. *Network Centric Warfare[electronic resource]: Department of Defense report to Congress.* (Washington D.C.: Office of the Secretary of Defense, 27 July 2001. http://www.dod.mil/nii/NCW/. pdf.), 11-1-6.

2 Ibid., 10-19.

3 Bradley, LCDR Carl M. *"INTELLIGENCE, SURVEILLANCE AND RECONNAISSANCE IN SUPPORT OFOPERATION IRAQI FREEDOM: CHALLENGES FOR RAPID MANEUVERS AND JOINT C4ISR INTEGRATION AND INTEROPERABILITY."* (Newport, Rl.: Naval War College, 9 Feb 2004.), 4.

4 Ibid., 4.

5 *Report of the Defense Science Board. Task Force on Command, Control, Communications, Computers, Intelligence, Surveillance and Reconnaissance (C4ISR).* (Washington D.C.: Office of the Under Secretary of Defense for Acquisition and Technology, February 1997.), 1.

6 Ibid.,1-2.

7 US. Congress. Senate. *Authorizing Appropriations for Fiscal Year 2004 for Intelligence and Intelligence-Related Activities of the United States Government, the Community Management Account, and the Central Intelligence Agency Retirement and Disability System. S. Rept 108-44,* (Washington D.C.: U.S. G.P.O., May 8 2003.), 13.

8 Cambone, Dr. Stephen A. *Statement of Dr. Stephen A Cambone Undersecretary of Defense for Intelligence Before the Senate Armed Services Committee Strategic Forces Subcommittee.,* (Washington D.C.: Office Of the Secretary of Defense, 7 April 2004.), 6.

9 Lambeth, Benjamin S. *NATO's Air War for Kosovo: A Strategic and Operational Assessment* Project Air Force Report. (Santa Monica, CA.: Rand, 2001.), 118.

10 Tirpak, John A. "ISR Miracles at a Reasonable Price." *Air Force Magazine Online,* February, 2006. http://www.afa.org/magazine/feb2006/0206ISR.asp

11 Pike, John for Federation of American Scientists. "Joint Airborne SIGINT Architecture (JASA)." November 21 1998. http://www.fas.org/irp/program/core/jasa.htm.

12 Zenker, David R. "Joint Working Group Maps Coherent Modernization." *Signal*, October 2001 http://www.afcea.org/signal/articles/anmviewer.asp?a=486&z=31.

13 US Congress., *House Report 108-354 – National Defense Authorization Act For Fiscal Year 2004 Sec. 923 Integration of Defense Intelligence, Surveillance and Reconnaissance Capabilities.,* (Washington D.C.: G.P.O., July 12 2005.)

14 Ackerman, Robert K., "Congress Cites Global Information Grid Challenges." *SIGNAL* 16 August 2004. http://www.imakenews.com/signal/e_article000290728.cfm.

15 Bolton Claude M. *Testimony Before the Subcommittee on Tactical Air and Land Forces Committee on Armed Services and House Permanent Select Committee on Intelligence United States House of Representatives on the Aerial Common Sensor.* , (Washington D.C.: Office of the Secretary of the Army, October 2005.), 2.

16 Ibid., 3.

17 Global Security. "Aerial Common Sensor" http://www.globalsecurity.org/intell/systems/acs.htm.

18 US Defense Science Board. *Report of the Defense Science Board Task Force on Concurrency and Risk of the F-22 Program.* (Washington D.C.: Office of the Under Secretary of

Defense for Acquisition and Technology, April 1995.), 24.

19 Quoted in Fabey, Michael. "Supersonic SIGINT (signals intelligence) is back: ISR sensors
   built into F/A-22, JSF fuselages." *C4ISR Journal,* 17 June 2005
   www.isrjournal.com/story.php?F=921293 (accessed 12 January 2005)..

20 Quoted in Fabey. "Supersonic SIGINT is back."

21 Fabey. "Supersonic SIGINT is back.".

22 Quoted in Fabey. "Supersonic SIGINT is back.".

23 Goodman Glen W. "Confluence of Missions: the Electronic Warfare and ISR domains begin
   to overlap." *C4ISR Journal*, 17 October 2005
   http://www.isrjournal.com/story.php?F=1041655 (accessed 15 February 2006)..

24 Ibid.

25 Ibid.

26 US Department of the Air Force. *The U.S. Air Force transformation flight plan 2004.*
   (Washington D.C.: Deputy Chief of Staff for Plans and Programs, 2004.), 67.

27 Ibid., 67.

28 US Department of Defense. *Quadrennial Defense Review.* (Washington D.C.: Department of
   Defense. 2006.), 55.

29 *Joint Vision 2020 America's Military: Preparing for Tomorrow.* (Washington D.C.: G.P.O.
   June, 2000), 8-11.

30 US Department of the Air Force. *The U.S. Air Force transformation flight plan 2004.*
   (Washington D.C.: Deputy Chief of Staff for Plans and Programs, 2004.), 55.

Bibliography:

Ackerman, Robert K., "Congress Cites Global Information Grid Challenges." *SIGNAL* 16 August 2004. http://www.imakenews.com/signal/e_article000290728.cfm.

Bradley, LCDR Carl M. *"INTELLIGENCE, SURVEILLANCE AND RECONNAISSANCE IN SUPPORT OFOPERATION IRAQI FREEDOM: CHALLENGES FOR RAPID MANEUVERS AND JOINT C4ISR INTEGRATION AND INTEROPERABILITY."* Newport, RI.: Naval War college, 9 Feb 2004.

Bolton Claude M. *Testimony Before the Subcommittee on Tactical Air and Land Forces Committee on Armed Services and House Permanent Select Committee on Intelligence United States House of Representatives on the Aerial Common Sensor.* , Washington D.C.: Office of the Secretary of the Army, October 2005.

Cambone, Dr. Stephen A. *Statement of Dr. Stephen A Cambone Undersecretary of Defense for Intelligence Before the Senate Armed Services Committee Strategic Forces Subcommittee.,* Washington D.C.: Office Of the Secretary of Defense, 7 April 2004.

Fabey, Michael. "Supersonic SIGINT (signals intelligence) is back: ISR sensors built into F/A-22, JSF fuselages." *C4ISR Journal,* 17 June 2005 www.isrjournal.com/story.php?F=921293 (accessed 12 January 2005).

Global Security. "Aerial Common Sensor" http://www.globalsecurity.org/intell/systems/acs.htm.

Goodman Glen W. "Confluence of Missions: the Electronic Warfare and ISR domains begin to overlap." *C4ISR Journal*, 17 October 2005 http://www.isrjournal.com/story.php?F=1041655 (accessed 15 February 2006).

Joint Vision 2020 America's Military: Preparing for Tomorrow. Washington D.C.: G.P.O. June, 2000.

Lambeth, Benjamin S. *NATO's Air War for Kosovo: A Strategic and Operational Assessment* Project Air Force Report. Santa Monica, CA.: Rand, 2001.

Pike, John for Federation of American Scientists. "Joint Airborne SIGINT Architecture (JASA)." November 21 1998. http://www.fas.org/irp/program/core/jasa.htm.

Report of the Defense Science Board. Task Force on Command, Control, Communications, Computers, Intelligence, Surveillance and Reconnaissance (C4ISR). Washington D.C.: Office of the Under Secretary of Defense for Acquisition and Technology, February 1997.

Tirpak, John A. "ISR Miracles at a Reasonable Price." *Air Force Magazine Online,* February, 2006. http://www.afa.org/magazine/feb2006/0206ISR.asp.

US Congress., *House Report 108-354 – National Defense Authorization Act For Fiscal Year 2004 Sec. 923 Integration of Defense Intelligence, Surveillance and Reconnaissance Capabilities.,* Washington D.C.: G.P.O., July 12 2005.

US. Congress. Senate. *Authorizing Appropriations for Fiscal Year 2004 for Intelligence and Intelligence-Related Activities of the United States Government, the Community Management Account, and the Central Intelligence Agency Retirement and Disability System. S. Rept 108-44,* Washington D.C.: U.S. G.P.O., May 8 2003.

US Defense Science Board. *Report of the Defense Science Board Task Force on Concurrency and Risk of the F-22 Program.* Washington D.C.: Office of the Under Secretary of Defense for Acquisition and Technology, April 1995.

US Department of the Air Force. *The U.S. Air Force transformation flight plan 2004.* Washington D.C.: Deputy Chief of Staff for Plans and Programs, 2004.

US Department of Defense. *Network Centric Warfare[electronic resource]: Department of Defense report to Congress.* Washington D.C.: Office of the Secretary of Defense, 27 July 2001. http://www.dod.mil/nii/NCW/. pdf (accessed 7 January 2006).

US Department of Defense. *Quadrennial Defense Review.* Washington D.C.: Department of Defense. 2006.

Zenker, David R. Joint "Working Group Maps Coherent Modernization." *Signal*, October 2001 http://www.afcea.org/signal/articles/anmviewer.asp?a=486&z=31.

CPSIA information can be obtained
at www.ICGtesting.com
Printed in the USA
BVOW04s0104020118
504178BV00011B/600/P